CREEPY, KOOKY SCIENCE

Eerie Science Experiments

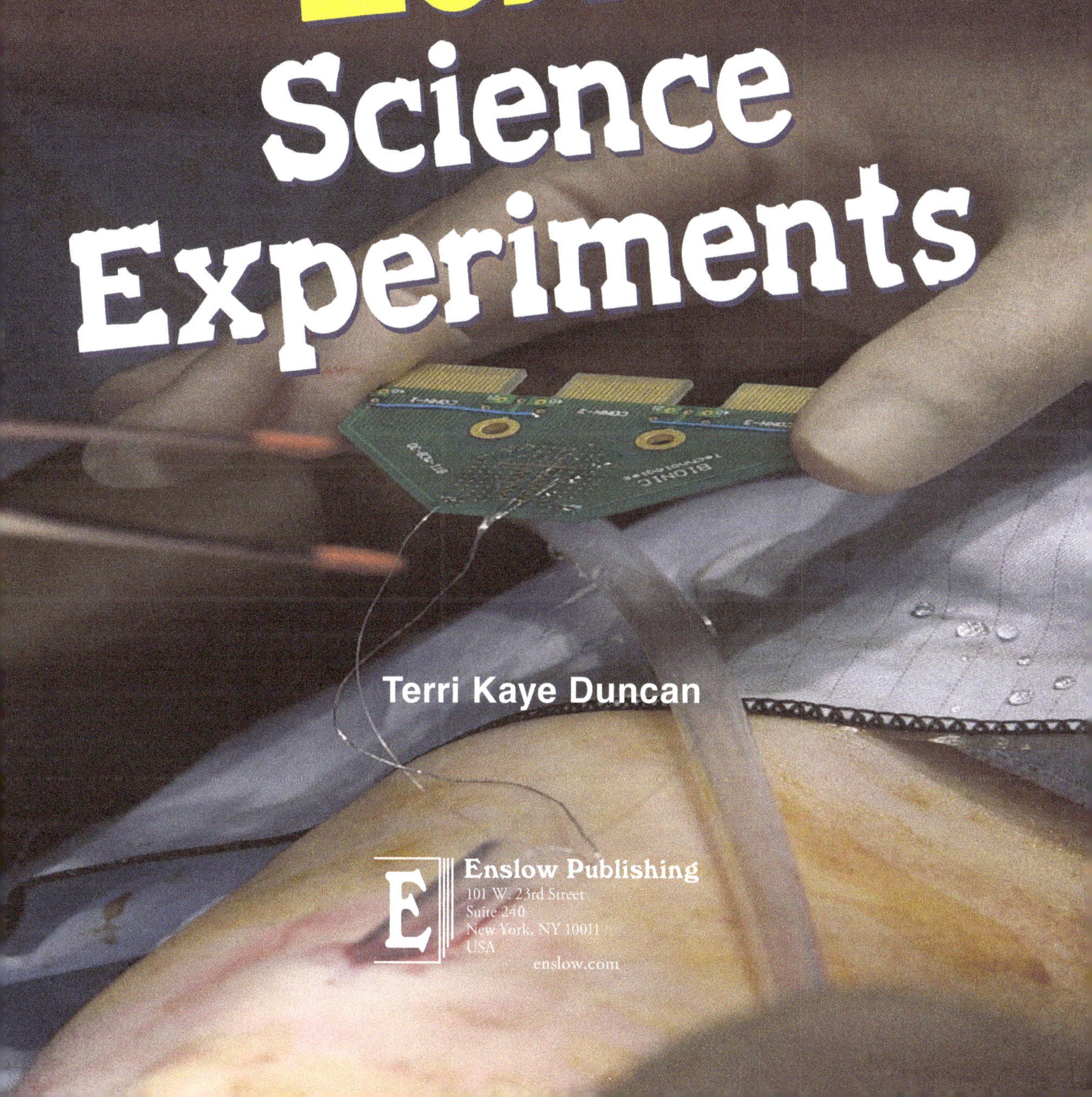

Terri Kaye Duncan

Enslow Publishing
101 W. 23rd Street
Suite 240
New York, NY 10011
USA
enslow.com

Published in 2020 by Enslow Publishing, LLC
101 W. 23rd Street, Suite 240, New York, NY 10011

Library of Congress Cataloging-in-Publication Data

Names: Duncan, Terri Kaye, author.
Title: Eerie science experiments / Terri Kaye Duncan.
Description: New York : Enslow Publishing, 2020. | Series: Creepy, kooky science | Audience: Grades 5 to 8. | Includes bibliographical references and index.
Identifiers: LCCN 2019004896| ISBN 9781978513754 (library bound) | ISBN 9781978513747 (pbk.)
Subjects: LCSH: Science—Experiments—Juvenile literature. | Science—History—Juvenile literature.
Classification: LCC Q164 .D86 2020 | DDC 507.8—dc23
LC record available at https://lccn.loc.gov/2019004896

Printed in the United States of America

To Our Readers: We have done our best to make sure all websites in this book were active and appropriate when we went to press. However, the author and the publisher have no control over and assume no liability for the material available on those websites or on any websites they may link to. Any comments or suggestions can be sent by email to customerservice@enslow.com.

Photo Credits: Eerie Science Experiments – Photo research by Bruce Donnola

Cover, pp. 1, 36 Tim Ockenden/PA Images/Getty Images; p. 5 Library of Congress Prints and Photographs Division; pp. 8, 10 Bettmann/Getty Images; p. 12 khlungcenter/Shutterstock.com; p. 14 AFP/Getty Images; p. 15 ullstein bild/Getty Images; p. 19 Education Images/Universal Images Group/Getty Images; pp. 20, 30 © AP Images; p. 22 Barcroft Media/Getty Images; p. 26 Kateryna Kon/Science Photo Library/Getty Images; p. 28 Sven Nackstrand/AFP/Getty Images; p. 31 Designua/Shutterstock.com; p. 37 Mark Runnacles/Getty Images

Contents

Introduction

Since the dawn of time, humans have learned from and about the world around them—building tools, discovering fire, inventing the wheel, considering whether the sun revolves around Earth or vice versa. When the ancient Greek philosopher Aristotle (384 BCE–322 BCE) began his scientific observations, he not only tried to find general agreement about a particular subject, but he also communicated his observations. He laid the groundwork for all those with curious minds who came later.

Observation, curiosity, and the desire to know more remain the basic building blocks of science. Science includes the things already known and the discovery of new knowledge through observation and experimentation. While experimenting, scientists follow very specific steps. Everything starts with a question. Then, they study what is already known about a certain topic. They develop a hypothesis based on existing research. A hypothesis is an idea that can be tested and either proven or disproven. The hypothesis must be tested through experimentation. The experiment results are studied. Sometimes, the results are exactly what the scientists predicted. Other times, the results are totally unexpected. Whatever the outcome, new knowledge is gained and can be shared.

Science experiments are not conducted randomly. They require a great deal of thought and preparation. Science experiments can be conducted in very controlled environments such as laboratories, or they can occur in real-life settings. Whether the experiment occurs in a lab or in a natural setting, it is very important that the scientist controls anything that can change the outcome of the experiment. These factors are called variables. The scientist must also be able to observe and measure so that exact data can be recorded. Personal opinions cannot affect the experiment.

In 1861, Louis Pasteur published his germ theory, which explained the relationship between germs and disease. This led to the development of vaccines for anthrax and rabies.

Many science experiments proceed exactly as the scientist expects. Louis Pasteur (1822–1895) was certain that food did not spoil because of bad air. After observing vats of beer that were going sour and studying them, he noticed bacteria. He then did a simple experiment to prove that these germs caused food to spoil. Pasteur's work changed the food and medicine industry forever. He set out to prove a hypothesis and did just that.

This is not always the case, however. There have been times when experiments have gone wrong. When Thomas Edison (1847–1931) was experimenting with electricity, he killed an elephant! Science experiments can also produce unexpected results. Alexander Fleming (1881–1955) did not set out to change modern medicine with the discovery of the first antibiotic. He was simply studying bacteria. Without accidents in the laboratory, this world may not have microwave ovens, Super Glue, or X-rays!

Some scientists are also willing to go to great lengths to test a hypothesis. Some of their methods, especially in the past, could be considered extreme and possibly even cruel. Though there are many rules in place today to protect the scientist as well as the test subjects, some scientists from days gone by conducted science experiments that were eerie, gross, and just plain unbelievable!

CHAPTER 1

What Comes Out Goes Back In

In 1793, Philadelphia, Pennsylvania, was a thriving city. Approximately fifty-five thousand people called the city home. Since 1790, the city had served as the temporary capital of the United States and was home to important people of the time, including George Washington.

Philadelphia's port was the busiest port in the country. During the summer of 1793, it was unusually hot and dry. Those conditions made the area around the port the perfect breeding ground for flies and mosquitos.

Yellow Fever Goes Viral

That summer, many of the ships arriving at the port were filled with refugees from the Caribbean who were escaping political unrest in their home countries. They brought with them a terrible illness. It caused fever with aches and pains, vomiting, bleeding, and eventually organ failure. In a short period of time, between August and November 1793, the mysterious virus killed almost 10 percent of the city's population.[1]

This woodcut shows a carriage picking up the dead and dying. During the yellow fever epidemic in 1793, people who could not leave Philadelphia stayed indoors and businesses closed, leaving doctors' carriages and hearses as the only vehicles on the streets.

The terrible disease was first reported in the United States in 1699. By 1740, doctors had a name for the virus: yellow fever. They named it this due to the yellow color of the skin and eyes of those affected by it. No one knew the cause of yellow fever, and no cure existed. As many as a hundred people a day died during the outbreak. Those with the ability to do so left the city in fear. Finally, after a cold front moved through Philadelphia in late October 1793, the outbreak subsided.[2]

Stubbins Ffirth Stresses His Observations

Stubbins Ffirth was just a boy during the deadly 1793 yellow fever outbreak, but he developed an interest in investigating the cause of the disease after becoming a medical student at the University of Pennsylvania in 1801. He observed that more people came down with the disease during the summer months. In the winter, the number of cases dropped. For this reason, he believed that the illness was a result of the stress caused by the summer heat. He did not believe that yellow fever was contagious. His mission was to prove his hypothesis.[3]

Ffirth thought that the best way to prove that yellow fever was not contagious was to come in contact with the bodily fluids of people infected with the disease. He selected those who were clearly ill and in the late stages of the virus. At first, he used animals to test his hypothesis. However, after five attempts injecting dogs and cats with vomit collected from infected patients did not produce satisfactory results, he decided he needed a human test subject. Ffirth selected himself![4]

Could the Answer Come Up in Vomit?

Ffirth went to great lengths to prove his hypothesis. He injected vomit in his veins.[5] He made cuts on his skin and smeared it over the incisions. When that failed to make him sick, the doctor in training poured the vomit into his eyeballs![6] Despite all of his efforts, he did not come down with yellow fever.

Ffirth was not through experimenting. He fried vomit in a pan and inhaled the steam. He even drank vomit! Nothing happened. When it became obvious that vomit was not going to cause him to contract yellow fever, he repeated some of the experiments on

In 1939, artist Dean Cornwall painted *Conquerors of Yellow Fever* to honor those whose scientific achievements conquered yellow fever, including Carlos Finlay (in the black suit with the white whiskers), Walter Reed (in the white uniform by the staircase), and James Carroll (in the center, being purposely infected with yellow fever for an experiment).

himself with urine, saliva, and even the blood from infected people. Still, nothing happened. Based on his gross experimentation, Ffirth confidently declared that his hypothesis was correct: yellow fever was not contagious.[7]

Ffirth died in 1820 believing his hypothesis about the disease was correct. He never learned that he was wrong. Some sixty years after Ffirth's death, Cuban scientist Carlos Finlay (1833–1915) determined that yellow fever is actually transmitted by mosquito bites.[8] Finlay's work was confirmed in 1900 by two United States Army physicians, James Carroll (1854–1907) and Walter Reed (1851–1902). Finally, in 1936, Max Theiler (1899–1972), a professor at Harvard University, developed a vaccine for the dreaded disease.[9]

Furthermore, the virus is contagious in its early stages. Yellow fever is carried from one human to another through the *Aedes aegypti* species of mosquito. The mosquito gets the virus from biting an infected person. Then the mosquito bites another

Mosquito Problems Persist

Mosquitoes are still a problem today. Zika is a virus spread by the bite of an infected *Aedes aegypti* or *Aedes albopictus* species of mosquito. It can bite an unsuspecting person during the day or at night.

Many people infected with Zika may not even realize they have the virus. Some people, however, can get a fever, have a rash, or experience muscle aches. A pregnant woman can spread the virus to her unborn baby. This can cause the baby to have medical problems or to die. There is no vaccine for Zika, but scientists are working on developing one.

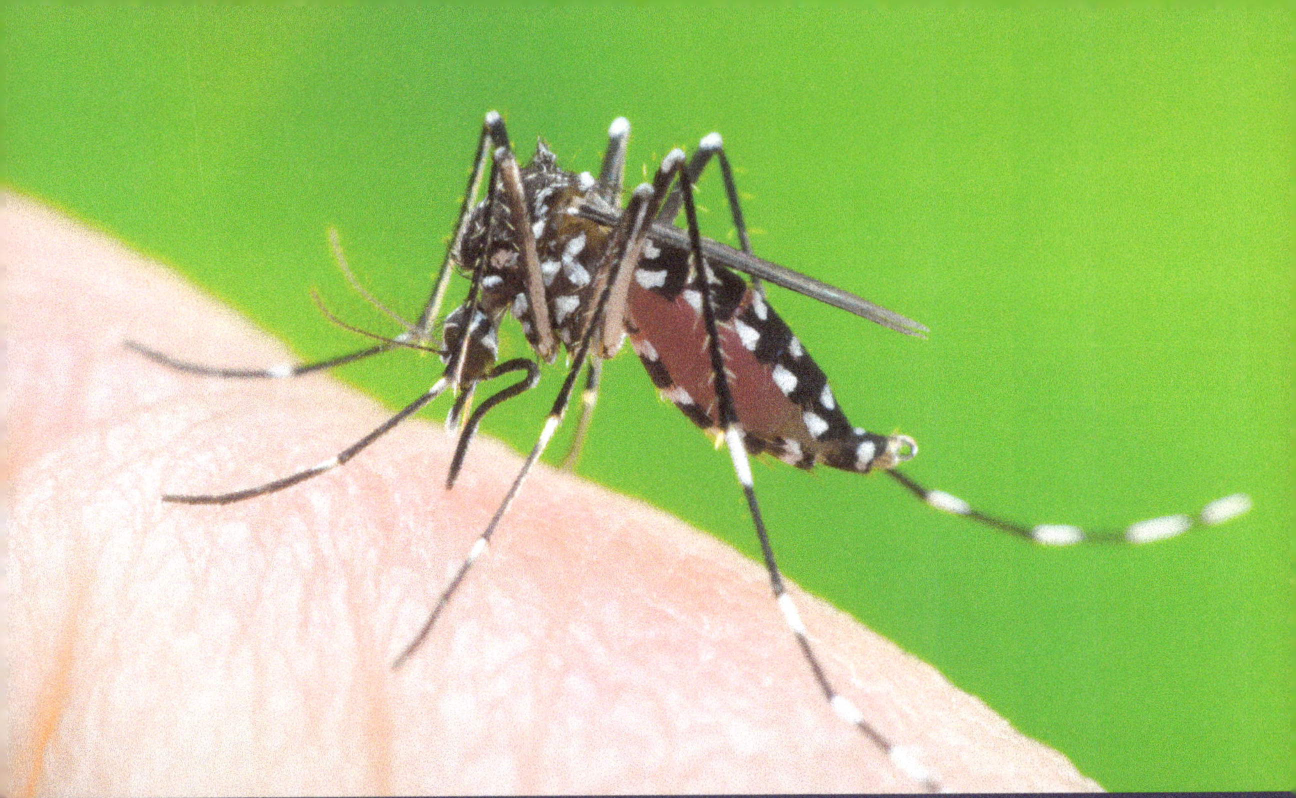

Each year, more than a million people around the world die as a result of diseases carried by mosquitoes such as *Aedes aegypti*.

person and transmits the virus to that human. The human who carries the disease is most infectious to the mosquito just before he or she develops a fever and for about five days after that.[10] Since Ffirth experimented with the bodily fluids of patients in late stages of the disease, he never contracted yellow fever despite drinking their vomit.

CHAPTER 2

Absolute Obedience

It is unlikely that many people, scientists or otherwise, would do what Stubbins Ffirth did and drink vomit to prove a hypothesis. However, experiments sometimes do require human test subjects. Today, there are many rules scientists must follow when conducting experiments, especially when testing on people is necessary. For instance, the scientist must treat the human test subject with respect. The experiment cannot cause harm to the person. When choosing test subjects, the scientist must be fair and impartial. The scientist must also keep very detailed records to show that all rules are being followed.

Many of the rules that now apply exist because of cruel treatment to humans during experiments and research conducted in the past. A series of psychological experiments conducted by a psychologist from Yale University during the 1960s falls into this category. His eerie experiments demonstrated the shocking power of authority and obedience to that authority.

Adolf Eichmann: Obey Without Question

During World War II, Adolf Eichmann (1906–1962) was a member of the Nazi Party and a high-ranking German soldier. In 1942, he was assigned the task of organizing the execution of Jewish people by identifying them, assembling them, and transporting them to concentration camps where millions met their deaths. When the war in Europe ended in 1945, Eichmann was captured and sent to a prison camp. However, he escaped. He was recaptured in Argentina in 1960. In April 1961, he was brought to trial for his war crimes.

During the trial, Eichmann denied having killed anyone. He argued that he was simply following

When former Nazi Adolf Eichmann, pictured here about 1960, was located in Argentina by agents from Israel's intelligence service, he was living in Buenos Aires and using the name Ricardo Klement.

orders and serving his country. When the trial ended, however, he was found guilty and sentenced to death.[1]

Stanley Milgram's Psychological Obedience Experiments

The Adolf Eichmann trial caught the attention of Yale University psychologist Stanley Milgram (1933–1984). He wondered what a person would be willing to do if he or she was ordered to do so by an authority figure. In order to find out, Milgram designed a scary looking machine to deliver electrical shocks. The generator was labeled with shock levels that started at 30 volts and went all the way up to 450 volts. The labels also had terms such as "slight shock" all the way up to "XXX." In truth, the "machine" was just a prop. It did not actually have the power to deliver an electrical shock.[2]

Next, Milgram placed an ad in the newspaper and hired forty

Stanley Milgram's shock experiment was enlightening, though many would question if it had gone too far by leading people to believe they were causing others harm. The rules concerning experimentation on people are much stricter now; Milgram would not have been allowed to do this experiment today.

Intelligent Disobedience

Seeing Eye dogs are taught to be the eyes and ears for their handlers. They are responsible for helping people with disabilities cross streets and avoid tripping hazards, and to alert them to changes in elevation such as curbs.

Though guide dogs must be trained to obey commands, they must also be taught when to refuse a command no matter what the handler says. This ability is called "intelligent disobedience." If the handler gives a command but the animal senses danger, then the dog must ignore the handler's command for their safety. This ability makes the guide dog invaluable!

men. These men became "teachers" in the experiment. Additionally, there were "students." The "students" were aware of the experiment and of the role they would play. The forty hired "teachers" were not told of the true nature of the experiment. Instead, they were led to believe that they were part of a "learning task." There was also an experimenter dressed in a gray lab coat who provided instructions. He, too, knew all about the experiment.[3]

The teachers and students were placed in separate rooms. The teacher was instructed to read a series of word pairs such as blue–girl or green–boy. The student was told to memorize the word pairs. Then, the teacher would call out one word from each pair. The student had to provide the paired word. If the student gave a wrong answer, then the teacher was told to punish the student by delivering an electric shock. The shock levels increased with each incorrect answer. If a teacher seemed reluctant to administer a shock, then the experimenter urged the teacher to continue because doing so was a requirement.[4]

Teachers were not aware that those acting as students were told to answer incorrectly. They also did not know that the students' screams and protests were not real. To the teachers, everything was very real and very disturbing.

The Shocking Results

Of the forty teachers, twenty-six obeyed all instructions. Even when the students cried out in pain, they delivered the maximum voltage. Though some of the teachers became very upset, they followed orders all the way to the end. The remainder stopped before reaching the highest shock level. Many of the participants acting as teachers experienced extreme anxiety. Some even asked to stop during the experiment but were not allowed to do so. Because of the extremely stressful situation in which they were involved, the teachers were told the truth after the experiment ended.[5]

Milgram's experiment showed that 65 percent of participants were willing to follow orders even if doing so brought physical harm to another. Some researchers questioned not only his results but also his methods. However, similar experiments conducted since then have had similar results. A comparable study with eighty participants conducted in Poland fifty years after Milgram's original experiment found that nearly 90 percent were willing to use the highest voltage![6] Now that is shocking!

CHAPTER 3

Brain Warfare

The brain has fascinated scientists for centuries. It is responsible for intelligence, and it is the control center for emotion, behavior, and body movement. This organ of the body in both animals and human subjects has been the focus of many scientific studies and experiments. Some have even investigated ways to control the mind!

In the early to mid-1900s, it was believed that the best way to treat mental illness and depression was to perform an operation on the brain called a lobotomy. The first lobotomies involved drilling a hole through the skull and into the front of the brain since the front of the brain controls behavior and emotion. A chemical was then injected into the brain to destroy the fibers connecting the front parts of the brain to the rest of the organ. Later procedures did not require drilling into the brain. Instead, an instrument that looked like an ice pick was used. It was inserted into the eye socket using a hammer-like instrument and moved side-to-side to destroy the connections.

Between the late 1940s to the early 1950s, between forty thousand and fifty thousand lobotomies were performed in the United States! Sadly, most did not have positive results. In fact, many patients experienced far greater mental issues after their surgeries. Some could no longer function on their own. Some patients died.

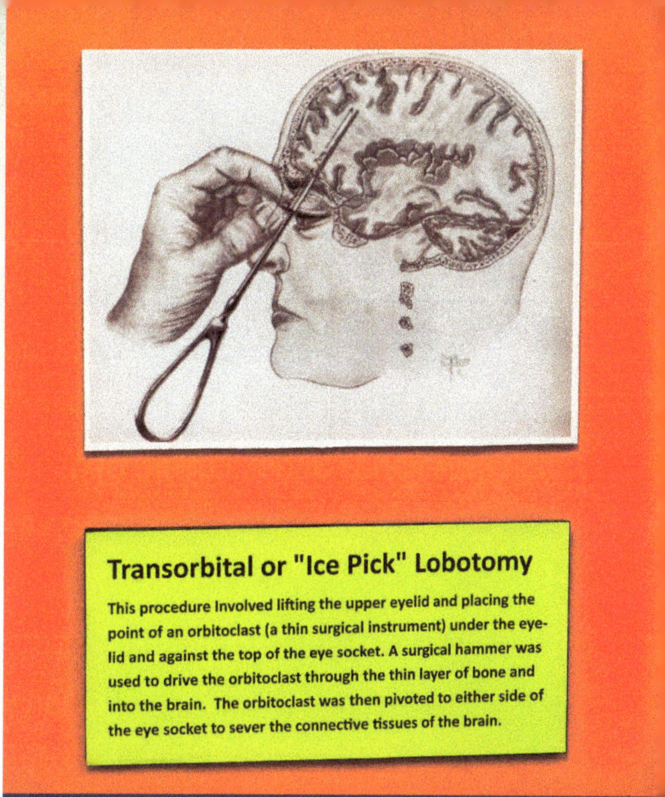

A display from the Glore Psychiatric Museum in Missouri shows an "ice pick" lobotomy. Dr. Walter Freeman, who developed the lobotomy technique of accessing the brain through an eye socket, had no surgical training and used an ice pick from his kitchen in early surgeries.

Stopping the Charge

José Delgado (1915–2011) intended to be an eye doctor like his father. However, the brain fascinated him. He believed that there had to be a safer way to treat mental illness than lobotomies. His idea was to control the way the brain worked using small devices implanted in the brain.[1]

Delgado, who was from Spain, was also quite the inventor. Using his medical skills and his technology skills, he developed a device that could be implanted in the brain. This device, called a stimoceiver, was controlled remotely by a handheld radio.[2]

In 1963, Delgado decided to test his stimoceiver on a fighting bull named Lucero. With the help of his wife as well as several assistants, Delgado implanted the device in Lucero's brain. Then, the brave scientist stepped into the bullring with the huge bull. Delgado waved his hands about. Lucero began to charge toward him! Delgado began pressing the buttons on the handheld remote device to send a radio signal to the implanted stimoceiver. Suddenly, when Lucero was just feet away from Delgado, the huge, angry animal stopped in a cloud of dust! Delgado then went behind a barrier for safety and stopped pressing the buttons. Lucero charged again, ramming the barrier![3] Delgado's stimoceiver and remote worked! He had stopped a charging bull!

Dr. José Delgado placed his life in jeopardy to test his stimoceiver by standing in front of a charging bull. In this November 3, 1966, photo, he holds a bull-fighter cape in one hand and his device in the other as the animal attacks.

Stimulating the Brain

Delgado did not just experiment on charging bulls. He tested his devices on dogs, cats, monkeys, and humans. With his stimoceivers, he was able to make his test subjects feel tired or more alert. He could also get them to smile, snarl, feel terror, or feel hungry.[4]

Over the years, Delgado also worked to develop devices that did not have to be implanted in the brain. He invented a halo-like device along with a helmet. It delivered electromagnetic pulses to specific areas of the brain. Delgado even tested this device on himself and his daughter![5]

While some scientists and medical experts were excited about Delgado's experiments; others were not. Some felt that his experiments could lead to mind control. In the 1950s and 1960s, he received funding for his experiments from the Office of Naval Intelligence, which

Top-Secret Mind-Control Experiment Is Not a Secret Anymore

Is it possible for one person or group to control the thoughts and beliefs of another? This process, often referred to as brainwashing or mind control, has been the subject of controversy for years. From 1953 until 1973, the CIA conducted a series of top-secret experiments on the topic through a program called MK-Ultra.

The original purpose of the program was to determine how certain chemical and biological materials affected human behavior. While some test subjects volunteered for the program, not all who participated were even aware they were doing so. The experiments included the use of hypnosis, radiation, and even illegal drugs!

was associated with the Central Intelligence Agency (CIA). People feared that if Delgado developed a reliable and predictable device, then governments and agencies such as the CIA would be able to control people with the push of a button.[6]

A Man Ahead of His Time

José Delgado set out to develop a more humane way to treat mental illness. However, his work was often the subject of controversy. Other scientists were suspicious of his intentions. There were some who

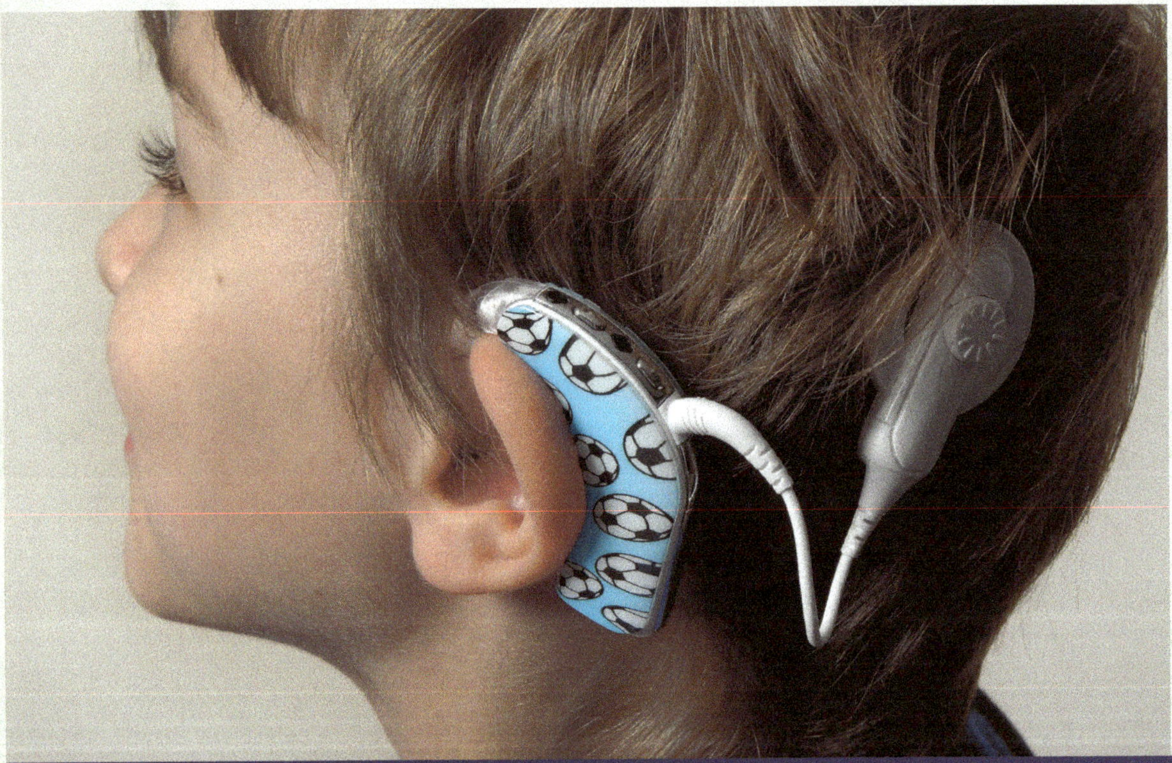

A cochlear implant is an electroceutical that helps a deaf person hear. A cochlear implant uses two parts: an internal receiver and an external speech processor. These work together to change sound into electrical signals that stimulate the hearing nerve.

believed that he was trying to develop methods to control people's thoughts remotely. Despite the critics, Delgado continued his work throughout his lifetime and encouraged experimentation in the field. "Can you avoid knowledge?" Delgado asked. "You cannot! Can you avoid technology? You cannot! Things are going to go ahead in spite of ethics, in spite of your personal beliefs, in spite of everything."[7]

Though his experiments were sometimes criticized, others admired him. His work helped lay the foundation for more research in the field. Today, devices such as those Delgado developed are referred to as electroceuticals or electrical microstimulation. These help treat diseases such as Parkinson's disease. Other devices are used to treat deafness and heart conditions. Electroceuticals could also one day replace the need for daily medications in illnesses such as arthritis and diseases of the intestines such as Crohn's disease.[8]

CHAPTER 4

Thirsting for a Stomach-Eating Germ Drink

For some scientists, getting others to believe their hypotheses proves to be the greatest challenge of all. This was certainly the case for Dr. Robin Warren (1937–) and Dr. Barry Marshall (1951–). The two Australian doctors tried for more than two years to convince others that the cause for stomach ulcers was not what the scientific and medical community believed for years. In order to prove their hypothesis and change long-held beliefs, Marshall went to extraordinary measures.

Marshall was an internist, which is a doctor who treats adults. For years, he had watched a number of his patients suffer with a painful stomach condition, ulcers. Some got so sick that they had to have their stomachs removed. Others died. Marshall knew that there had to be a better treatment than what was traditionally available. He was determined to prove it.

Why Worry About Stomach Ulcers?

Stomach ulcers are very painful sores in the lining of the stomach. The stomach has a thick layer of mucus to protect it from digestive juices that contain a great deal of acid. When the mucus layer is reduced, the acids begin to eat away at the tissues lining the stomach. This results in stomach ulcers.

People with stomach ulcers, also called peptic ulcers, often have pain in their stomachs. They often feel nauseous and do not have an appetite. They may also burp frequently and lose weight. While some ulcers may heal, others may not. Untreated ulcers can lead to very serious problems. They can cause internal bleeding or even eat a hole through the lining of the stomach. If this happens, a serious infection can develop.

Nobody's Listening

For years, doctors believed that stomach ulcers were caused by stress and lifestyle choices. People who smoked and those who lived in poor areas also seemed to develop ulcers more often than nonsmokers and those living in better economic conditions. Doctors often prescribed medicine to patients that helped ease the pain and heal the ulcers. However, the ulcers often returned.[1]

Marshall watched too many of his patients suffer. He was certain that the cause of stomach ulcers was not related to stress. Instead, he believed that the cause was a corkscrew-shaped bacterium called *Helicobacter pylori*. Dr. Robin Warren had discovered this bacterium in ulcer patients in 1982. The two men teamed up and studied the bacteria. They determined that it was not only connected to ulcers. It was also found in patients with stomach cancer. They also knew that the cure was antibiotics. However, other doctors were not convinced. They still believed that stress and lifestyle choices caused ulcers.[2]

Marshall and Warren could grow the bacteria in the lab. They could also show that patients with ulcers had the bacteria in their stomachs. Proving that it actually caused ulcers in people was another matter. The two doctors tried to grow the bacteria in mice.

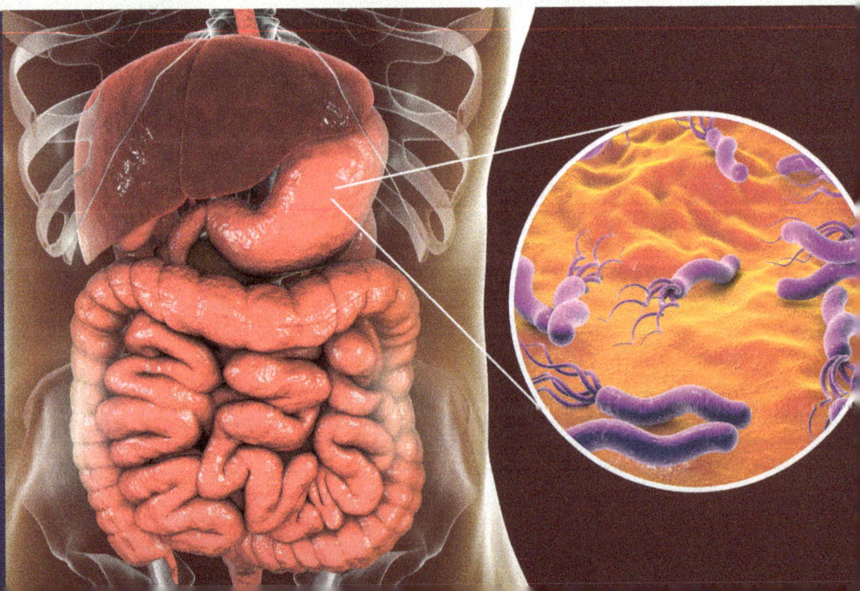

It is believed that *Helicobacter pylori* affects at least 50 percent of the world's population and is the greatest risk factor for stomach cancer, the second deadliest cancer in the world.

However, the mice were not affected, and there were now rules that did not allow scientists to experiment on people. The two doctors were in a dilemma.[3]

Proving Their Point

While Marshall and Warren could not experiment on other human test subjects, the rules did not say they could not experiment on their own bodies. In desperation, Marshall volunteered for the task! First, he underwent a medical procedure to prove that no *Helicobacter pylori* were growing in his stomach. Then, he made a special drink that contained the bacteria that was grown in the lab. Marshall guzzled it down![4]

Within five days of drinking the bacterial brew, Marshall began experiencing symptoms of an ulcer including vomiting and loss of appetite. He underwent yet another medical procedure to determine whether the bacteria were present in his stomach. They were everywhere! He treated himself with antibiotics. With that treatment, the ulcer disappeared![5]

Glowing Results

Glow-in-the-dark pigs and other animals are not science fiction. They are very real and help scientists learn more about diseases and develop treatments for those illnesses, so scientists don't have to experiment on themselves like Marshall did! Scientists use a protein from certain jellyfish, green fluorescent protein (GFP), and inject it into pig embryos. The result is that the pig's organs and skin glow under black light. This allows the scientists to see individual cells in action, something that would not be possible even with a microscope, since individual proteins in the cells are so small.

The piglets are not harmed by the GFP. Their lifespans are the same as pigs that do not glow in the dark!

Dr. Barry Marshall and Dr. Robin Warren attend a press conference on December 7, 2005, three days before they were jointly awarded a Nobel Prize in Physiology or Medicine in Stockholm, Sweden.

The two doctors shared their results. However, the medical community was still not convinced. Finally, in the mid-1990s, more than ten years after Marshall subjected himself to the experimentation, the findings were accepted. Doctors now know that *Helicobacter pylori* cause ulcers and that the bacteria can be spread through direct contact with bodily fluids such as saliva and vomit. It can also be spread through contaminated food or water. Antibiotics are now the preferred treatment for stomach ulcers.

In 2005, Warren and Marshall were awarded the Nobel Prize for their work. This award is a huge international honor. Only six Nobel Prizes are awarded internationally each year. Their willingness to do whatever it took to prove their hypothesis proved to be worth the effort after all!

CHAPTER 5

My, What a Big Ear You Have!

In 1818, Mary Shelley (1797–1851) published the book *Frankenstein*. The main character in the tale is Victor Frankenstein. He is a scientist who is fascinated by the creation of life. He studies the subject and discovers what he believes is the secret of life. Using old body parts, he creates a huge, horrible-looking creature. When the monster indeed comes to life, even the scientist is horrified by what he created!

The idea for the book came to Shelley through a dream. However, the idea that new body parts can be created in a lab is not a dream, nor is it a work of fiction. It is happening, and the first result was bizarre!

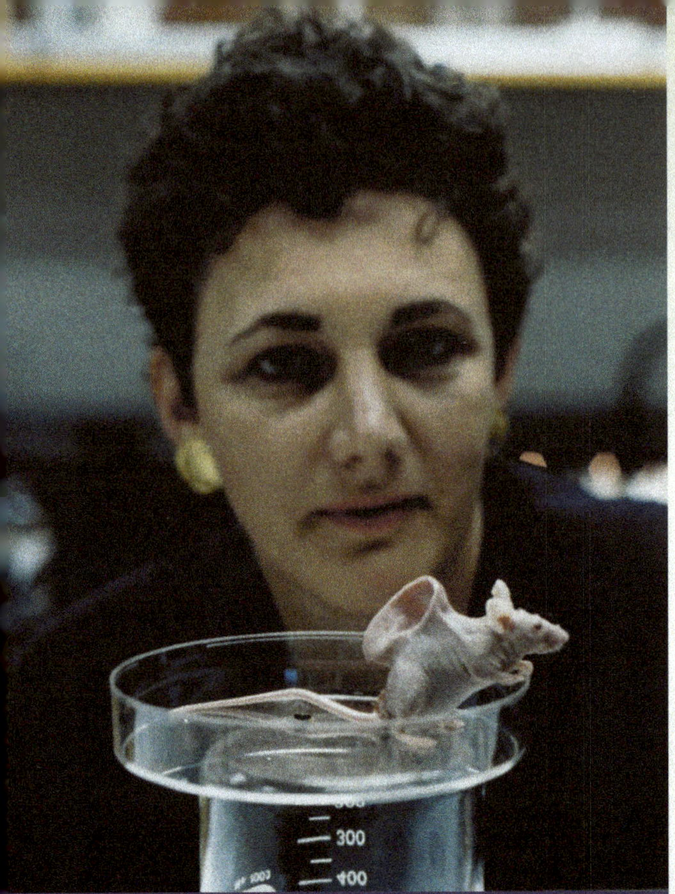

A BBC reporter looks at a mouse with an ear on its back in 1995. The Vacanti mouse was a nude mouse. A nude mouse does not have a normal thymus gland and has a defective immune system due to a genetic mutation.

Not Your Average Mouse

Euriculosaurus was just a mouse. He did look a bit different from other mice because he had no hair. That is simply the way he was born. He was also born with no real immune system. What made him very unique, though, was the human ear growing out of his back! He definitely was not born with that!

The mouse with the ear on his back was part of a project started in 1989 by Dr. Charles Vacanti. He is a surgeon and scientist who studies tissue engineering. Tissue engineering combines the use of living cells with engineering methods to grow new living tissue. Vacanti was drawn to this subject because as a doctor, he realized that there were not enough donor organs or tissue for patients who needed transplants or repairs.

Vacanti had an idea. He could build a frame, or scaffold, out of a special surgical material that would dissolve over time. On this scaffold, he would place cells from living tissue. Once these cell "seeds" were "planted" and placed in the proper conditions, they would begin to multiply. They would eventually fill up the scaffold and start growing into three-dimensional tissue. This could then be placed in or on the human body. Blood vessels would naturally grow into the new tissue, the scaffold would melt away, and the new tissue would blend into the old![1]

No Genetic Engineering Involved

When many people first saw a picture of the hairless mouse with a human ear growing out of its back, they were horrified. What kind of mad scientist would create such a monster? They believed that Vacanti changed an animal's DNA to create a new creature. DNA is the recipe book for a living thing. It is found in cells. DNA carries all of the instructions about how a living thing will look and function.

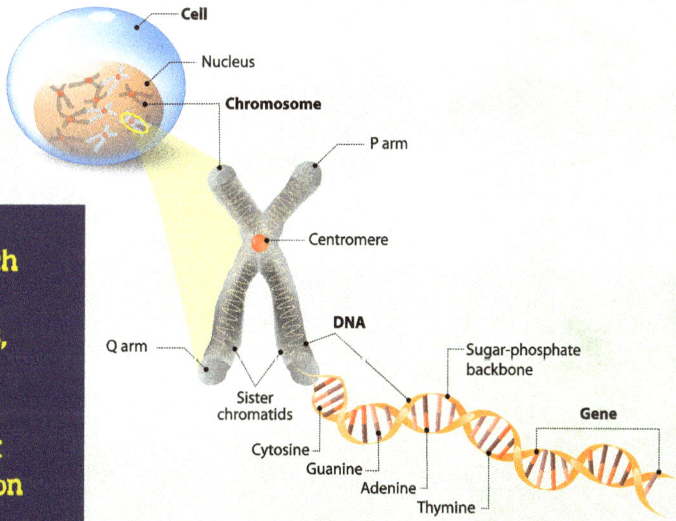

Genes are made up of DNA, which is packaged into chromosomes, located in the center, or nucleus, of a cell. If the strands of DNA from all the cells in the human body were placed end to end, it would stretch more than 110 billion miles (177 billion kilometers)!

A Smelly Problem

Cows belch and cows fart. When they do this, they give off large amounts of a smelly gas called methane. Methane is a greenhouse gas and is a threat to the planet's climate. In the United States alone, beef cattle produce as much methane as 24 million cars produce in a single year! Scientists discovered the bacterium that causes cows to produce methane. They also determined that a cow's genes play a role in the production of this bacterium. Through a genetic modification process called selective breeding, scientists hope to breed a line of cattle that produces less methane.

When scientists take DNA of one organism and add it into the DNA of another living thing, a new organism develops. This new creation is called a genetically modified organism (GMO). The process used is a type of genetic engineering. Genetic engineering can be done on bacteria, plants, or animals. It is most often used today to create new food crops.[2]

There was no genetic engineering involved in the mouse–ear project, however. Euriculosaurus simply had to hold up the scaffold that was seeded with cells from the knee of a cow. Though the scaffold was in the shape of a human ear, absolutely no human cells were used in the experiment. After the cells began to multiply, the scaffold was placed just under the mouse's skin. Because the mouse had no immune system, the mouse's body would not reject the new cells. Over a period of three months, extra blood vessels grew into the structure. These helped "feed" the cells as they multiplied. By the time the scaffold dissolved, the new tissue was strong enough to support itself.[3] Vacanti demonstrated that it was possible to grow new tissue thanks to Euriculosaurus.

The Growth of Tissue Engineering

On average, twenty people a day die waiting for an organ transplant. Every ten minutes, another name is added to a waiting list for an organ transplant. Additionally, there are thousands of others in need of new tissue due to injury or disease.[4] Perhaps the solution to the shortage lies in tissue engineering. Vacanti said he hopes that human tissue can one day be manufactured as easily as cell phones.[5] The engineered tissue could be used to replace bone, skin, or arteries.

That little mouse with an ear on his back carried a heavy load. Some people accused Vacanti and his team of creating a "Frankenmouse" with his strange experiment.[6] As it turns out, they were simply pioneers in a new field, one that has the potential to improve and save lives.

CHAPTER 6

The Human Cyborg

Imagine an organism that is part human and part machine. This organism would be considered a cyborg. Though cyborgs sound like characters in a science fiction movie, they are not. Right now, cyborgs are walking among us!

For centuries, scientists have been interested in replacing human body parts with technological devices. In 1958, Dr. Jack Steele (1924–2009), a doctor and Air Force colonel, invented a term for such studies: bionics. Bionics combines biology with technology.

Steele's work on bionics captured the attention of writer Martin Caidin (1927–1997). In 1972, Caidin wrote a book about a test pilot severely injured in a crash. The pilot's damaged body parts are replaced with mechanical parts that are far more powerful than his regular body parts. The book, *Cyborg*, inspired the television series

The Six Million Dollar Man. With that television series, the term "bionics" became a household word.

Though the television series was not entirely accurate in how it presented bionics, it did bring more attention to the topic. However, Professor Kevin Warwick (1954–) demonstrated in real life that a human cyborg was not just a fictional character. He even put his own body on the operating table to prove it!

Captain Cyborg

In 1998, Warwick began work on Project Cyborg. His goal was to develop a way for the human nervous system to communicate with computer systems. In order to demonstrate that this was possible, he had a silicon chip transponder surgically placed in his left arm. A transponder is a wireless device that picks up signals and automatically responds to them. The chip was just over 1 inch (2.5 centimeters) in diameter. During the surgery, Warwick remained awake. He needed to be able to talk to the doctors while they implanted the device into a nerve in his forearm. The surgery was risky. If something went wrong, there was the possibility of infection, amputation, or even brain damage.[1]

Fortunately, the procedure was successful. The chip gave off radio frequency signals. This allowed Warwick to interact with his surroundings. With the chip in place, the professor could "communicate" with the computer in the office. This allowed him to turn

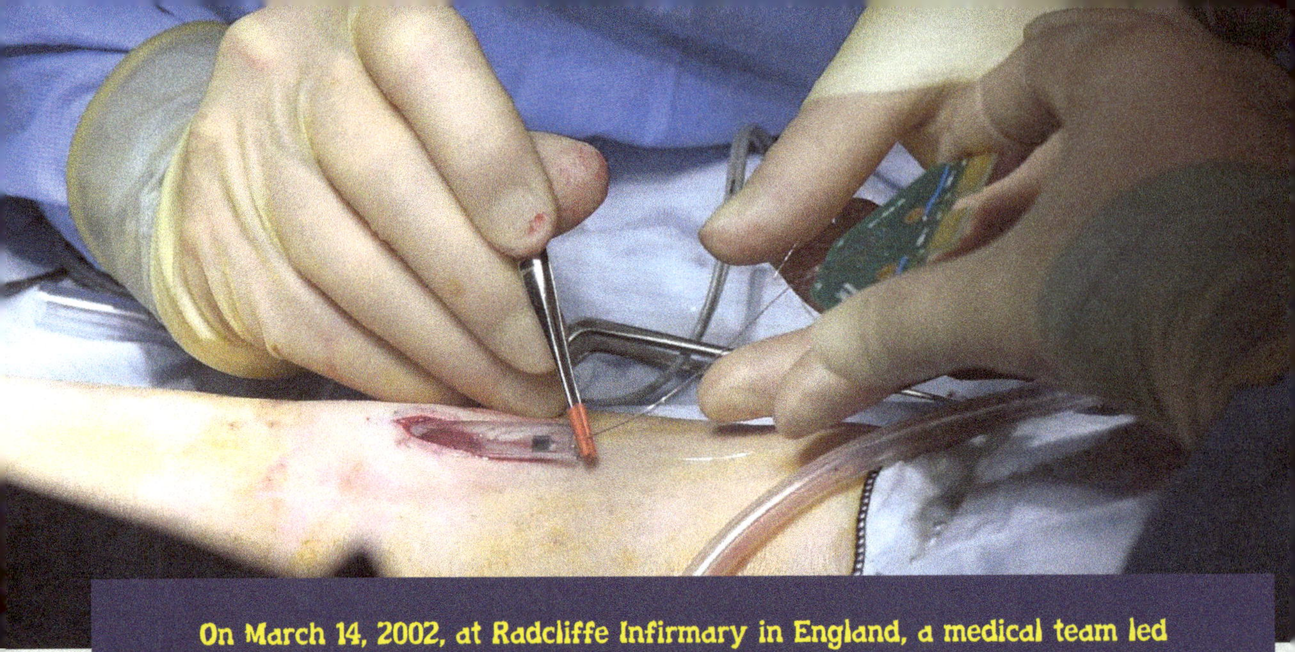

On March 14, 2002, at Radcliffe Infirmary in England, a medical team led by Dr. Amjad Shad and Dr. Peter Teddy surgically implanted electrodes into Kevin Warwick's left forearm so he could be hooked up to a computer.

lights on and off without having to touch a switch. Doors automatically opened for him. Even the telephone greeted him with, "Hello Professor Warwick."[2] The bionic implant was a success!

Professor Warwick was far from finished with his experiments, though. In 2002, phase two of Project Cyborg began. This time, he wanted to send signals from his own nervous system to a computer. Once again, he went to the operating table and stayed awake. This time, electrodes were placed in nerve fibers in his left arm. The implanted device was called BrainGate. Later, Warwick was plugged into a computer. The computer monitored the nerve signals from his brain to his arm. It also transmitted the signals as radio waves. Not only could he control his own arm, but he could also control a robotic arm that was across the ocean![3] Captain Cyborg was real!

Advancing the Future

Warwick was willing to experiment on himself in order to advance his research. Thanks to his work and the work of others, bionics are now being used in ways that once seemed impossible. This is certainly true in the area of prosthetics. Prosthetics are artificial devices that can replace damaged or missing arms, legs, and other body parts. Originally, prosthetics were made of wood or metal. They were often shaped to look like this missing limb, but they could be heavy and uncomfortable.

A nine-year-old boy receives a bionic hand. Electrodes placed under the skin pick up changes in the electrical patterns when muscles contract. Signals are sent to a microprocessor that tells the prosthetic hand to open and close.

The Buzz About Cyborg Beetles

The United States military had a mission for scientists. Develop tiny flying robots that could be used in dangerous territory. Additionally, they wanted to use live insects. Engineers at the University of California, Berkeley, accepted the mission! Engineers selected the flower beetle, a fierce-looking beetle almost 2 inches (5 cm) long with a hard outer shell. They developed a tiny system of implants and a separate remote. This allowed the engineers to wirelessly send signals to the beetle's brain and command it to take off, turn left or right, or hover in midflight. Cyborg beetles—part beetle, part machine—may be the military's newest recruits!

Today, prosthetics are made of more lightweight materials. They are custom fitted for comfort. Scientists also use bionics in prosthetics. Bionic arms use electricity and robotics to allow the user to operate the mechanical limb. In the near future, it may even be possible for nerve detectors to control the prosthetic. With this, a sensor would pick up a nerve signal from the spinal cord. The user would then be able to move the prosthetic device simply by imagining the movement![4]

Bionics are also being used to assist people with spinal cord injuries. Often, people with such injuries are unable to walk. Robotic exoskeletons may change this. A robotic exoskeleton is literally a power suit. The user wears it outside the body. It has motorized parts that can help the wearer with mobility and can also help him or her regain strength. It may look like something out of a Hollywood movie, but the robotic exoskeleton is already helping patients get out of wheelchairs and walk![5]

The Future Is Near

Professor Warwick sees a future where medicine is not the only way to treat physical and mental illness. Instead, electrical engineering can be used. This method is already being used to help control the tremors associated with Parkinson's disease.

Warwick also believes that artificial intelligence (AI) will play a larger role in the future. AI involves the development of machines that are able to perform tasks that normally involve human intelligence. Self-driving cars are on the roads today. Voice-recognition devices such as Siri and Alexa are in the hands of people everywhere. People also use AI devices to help schedule appointments, control the temperature in their homes, and select music or movies.[6]

Will robots lead the world one day and make important decisions? Warwick believes in that possibility. He is still working today to prove that robots and AI will have capabilities and abilities that go beyond what the human mind is capable of. He is even willing to go back to the operating table to test a brain implant to get there![7]

Chapter Notes

Chapter 1. What Comes Out Goes Back In

1. History.com editors, "Yellow Fever Breaks Out in Philadelphia," History, August 21, 2018, https://www.history.com/this-day-in-history/yellow-fever-breaks-out-in-philadelphia.
2. History.com editors.
3. Sankalan Baidya, "15 Interesting Stubbins Ffirth Facts," Facts Legend, March 29, 2015, https://factslegend.org/15-interesting-stubbins-ffirth-facts/.
4. Alpha History, "1804: Med Student Tests Theory by Drinking Black Vomit," Alpha History, 2016, https://alphahistory.com/pastpeculiar/1804-med-student-drinking-black-vomit/.
5. Alpha History.
6. Baidya.
7. Baidya.
8. "The History of Vaccines," the College of Physicians of Philadelphia, 2019, https://www.historyofvaccines.org/timeline#EVT_100407.
9. "The History of Vaccines."
10. "Transmission of Yellow Fever Virus," Centers for Disease Control, January 15, 2019, https://www.cdc.gov/yellowfever/transmission/index.html.

Chapter 2. Absolute Obedience

1. Lily Rothman, "*Operation Finale* Shows the Capture of Nazi Adolf Eichmann. But What Happened at His Trial Changed

History, Too," *Time*, August 29, 2018, http://time.com/5377670/operation-finale-adolf-eichmann-trial/.

2. Kendra Cherry, "Milgram's Experiments and the Perils of Obedience," Very Well Mind, November 19, 2018, https://www.verywellmind.com/the-milgram-obedience-experiment-2795243.
3. Cherry.
4. John Greenwood, "How Would People Behave in Milgram's Experiment Today?" Behavioral Scientist, July 24, 2018, http://behavioralscientist.org/how-would-people-behave-in-milgrams-experiment-today/.
5. Cherry.
6. Society for Personality and Social Psychology, "Conducting the Milgram Experiment in Poland, Psychologists Show People Still Obey," ScienceDaily, March 14, 2017, www.sciencedaily.com/releases/2017/03/170314081558.htm.

Chapter 3. Brain Warfare

1. John Horgan, "Tribute to José Delgado, Legendary and Slightly Scary Pioneer of Mind Control," *Scientific American*, September 25, 2017, https://blogs.scientificamerican.com/cross-check/tribute-to-jose-delgado-legendary-and-slightly-scary-pioneer-of-mind-control/.
2. Horgan.
3. Timothy Marzullo, "The Missing Manuscript of Dr. José Delgado's Radio Controlled Bulls," National Center for Biotechnology Information, June 15, 2017, https://www.ncbi.nlm.nih.gov/pmc/articles/PMC5480854/.
4. Horgan.
5. Horgan.

6. "1950s: Jose Delgado, MD, Pioneered Wireless Implanted Electrode to Control Human Behavior," Alliance for Human Research Protection, http://ahrp.org/ 1950s-jose-delgado-md-pioneered-wireless-implanted-electrode-to-control-human-behavior/ (accessed January 14, 2019).
7. Horgan.
8. Geoffrey Ling and Corinna Lanthan, "Electroceuticals: Nerve-Stimulating Therapies Could Soon Replace Drugs for Many Chronic Conditions," *Scientific American*, September 14, 2018, https://www.scientificamerican.com/article/electroceuticals/.

Chapter 4. Thirsting for a Stomach-Eating Germ Drink

1. Susan Erasmus, "The Real Cause of Stomach Ulcers," Health 24, December 18, 2017, https://www.health24.com/Medical/Heartburn/Helicobacter-pylori/Stomach-ulcers-the-real-cause-20120721.
2. Pamela Weintraub, "The Doctor Who Drank Infectious Broth, Gave Himself an Ulcer, and Solved a Medical Mystery," *Discover*, April 8, 2010, http://discovermagazine.com/2010/mar/07-dr-drank-broth-gave-ulcer-solved-medical-mystery.
3. Weintraub.
4. Barry Marshall and Paul Adams, "*Helicobacter pylori*: A Nobel Pursuit?" National Center for Biotechnology Information, November 22, 2008, https://www.ncbi.nlm.nih.gov/pmc/articles/PMC2661189/.
5. Weintraub.

Chapter 5. My, What a Big Ear You Have!

1. Karl Kruszelnicki, "Mouse with Human Ear," ABC Science, June 2, 2006, http://www.abc.net.au/science/articles/2006/06/02/1644154.htm.
2. Marc Lallanilla, "GMOs: Facts About Genetically Modified Food," Live Science, January 11, 2016, https://www.livescience.com/40895-gmo-facts.html.
3. Kruszelnicki.
4. "Facts and Myths," American Transplant Foundation, https://www.americantransplantfoundation.org/about-transplant/facts-and-myths/ (accessed January 17, 2019).
5. Kristin Hugo, "Exclusive: Whatever Happened to the Mouse with the Ear on Its Back?" *Newsweek*, September 16, 2017, https://www.newsweek.com/tissue-surgeon-ear-mouse-human-organs-transplant-cell-phones-666082.
6. Kruszelnicki.

Chapter 6. The Human Cyborg

1. Thomas Macaulay, "Meet Captain Cyborg: The Man That Biohacked His Own Body," Tech World, May 24, 2017, https://www.techworld.com/apps-wearables/professor-cyborg-reveals-secrets-of-cybernetic-communication-3659400/.
2. Macaulay.
3. Macaulay.
4. Fishadmin, "Top 5 Advances in Prosthetics in 2017," Fish Insurance, April 18, 2017, https://www.fishinsurance.co.uk/thehub/categories/prosthetics/top-5-advances-in-prosthetics-in-2017/.

5. Stephen Ashley, "Robotic Exoskeletons Are Changing Lives in Surprising Ways," NBC News, February 21, 2017, https://www.nbcnews.com/mach/innovation/robotic-exoskeletons-are-changing-lives-surprising-ways-n722676.
6. Farhan Saeed, "9 Powerful Examples of Artificial Intelligence in Use Today," IQVIS, January 16, 2017, https://www.iqvis.com/blog/9-powerful-examples-of-artificial-intelligence-in-use-today/.
7. Aurel Dragan, "BR Exclusive! Kevin Warwick: In 10-15 Years We Will Have Robots with Human-Size Brains," Business Review, October 17, 2018, http://business-review.eu/br-exclusive/br-exclusive-kevin-warwick-in-10-15-years-we-will-have-robots-with-human-size-brains-187977.

Glossary

authority figure A person in a position of power over others.

contagious Able to be spread from one living thing to another, usually through contact.

electrode A device that can carry electricity.

embryo An unborn baby that is still developing.

greenhouse gas A gas in the air that traps heat and causes warming of Earth's surface and the air above it.

hypothesis An idea that can be tested using experiments to prove that it is correct or that it is incorrect.

impartial Treating all equally and not favoring one over another.

implant To place a medical device or substance in the human body usually during a surgical procedure.

psychological experiment An experiment that uses human participants to study such topics as memory, emotion, and learning, as well as many other subjects dealing with human nature and human interactions.

scaffold A temporary structure.

selective breeding The process of choosing an adult male and an adult female with certain characteristics, and then breeding them so that the offspring will have those chosen characteristics.

transponder A wireless device that picks up signals and automatically responds to them.

Further Reading

Books

Baker, Theo. *Human Bodies*. Vero Beach, FL: Rourke Educational Media, 2018.

Drimmer, Stephanie Warren. *Ultimate Secrets Revealed: A Closer Look at the Weirdest, Wildest Facts on Earth*. Washington, DC: National Geographic Children's Books, 2018.

Rhatigan, Joe. *Wacky Inventions of the Future: Weird Inventions That Seem Too Crazy to Be Real!* Lake Forest, CA: Walter Foster Jr., 2019.

Young, Karen Romano. *Try This Extreme: 50 Fun & Safe Experiments for the Mad Scientist in You*. Washington, DC: National Geographic Children's Books, 2017.

Websites

National Geographic Kids: Science

www.natgeokids.com/uk/category/discover/science/

Explore topics in biology, astronomy, physics, and more.

Science Kids: Weird Science for Kids

www.sciencekids.co.nz/weird.html

Learn strange facts, watch fascinating videos, and conduct weird experiments.

Science News for Students

www.sciencenewsforstudents.org

Keep up with the latest science news on this site, which covers topics from the brain and body to careers in science and related fields.

Index